T0000718

To my dad, mushroom forager —K.G.
To my Papa Joe, wise like a mushroom —S.G.

A special thanks to mycologist Keith Seifert for his expert review.

Text copyright © 2024 by Kallie George
Illustrations copyright © 2024 by Sara Gillingham

24 25 26 27 28 5 4 3 2 1

All rights reserved. No part of this book may be reproduced, stored in a retrieval system or transmitted, in any form or by any means, without the prior written consent of the publisher or a license from The Canadian Copyright Licensing Agency (Access Copyright). For a copyright license, visit accesscopyright.ca or call toll free to 1-800-893-5777.

Greystone Kids / Greystone Books Ltd.
greystonebooks.com

Cataloguing data available from Library and Archives Canada
ISBN 978-1-77840-077-3 (cloth)
ISBN 978-1-77840-078-0 (epub)

Editing by Tiffany Stone
Copy editing and proofreading by Lisa Frenette
Cover and interior design by Sara Gillingham Studio
The illustrations in this book were rendered with a stylus, iPad, and computer.

Printed and bound in China on FSC® certified paper at Shenzhen Reliance Printing.
The FSC® label means that materials used for the product have been responsibly sourced.

Greystone Books thanks the Canada Council for the Arts, the British Columbia Arts Council, the Province of British Columbia through the Book Publishing Tax Credit, and the Government of Canada for supporting our publishing activities.

Canada

FSC
www.fsc.org
MIX
Paper from
responsible sources
FSC® C102842

BRITISH
COLUMBIA

BRITISH COLUMBIA
ARTS COUNCIL
An agency of the Province of British Columbia

Canada Council
for the Arts

Conseil des arts
du Canada

Greystone Books gratefully acknowledges the xʷməθkʷəy̓əm (Musqueam), Sḵwx̱wú7mesh (Squamish), and səlilwətaɬ (Tsleil-Waututh) peoples on whose land our Vancouver head office is located.

Kallie George + Sara Gillingham

MUSHROOMS KNOW

Wisdom From Our Friends the Fungi

GREYSTONE KIDS

GREYSTONE BOOKS • VANCOUVER/BERKELEY/LONDON

Mushrooms always wear their thinking caps.
They know so many things.

What do mushrooms know?

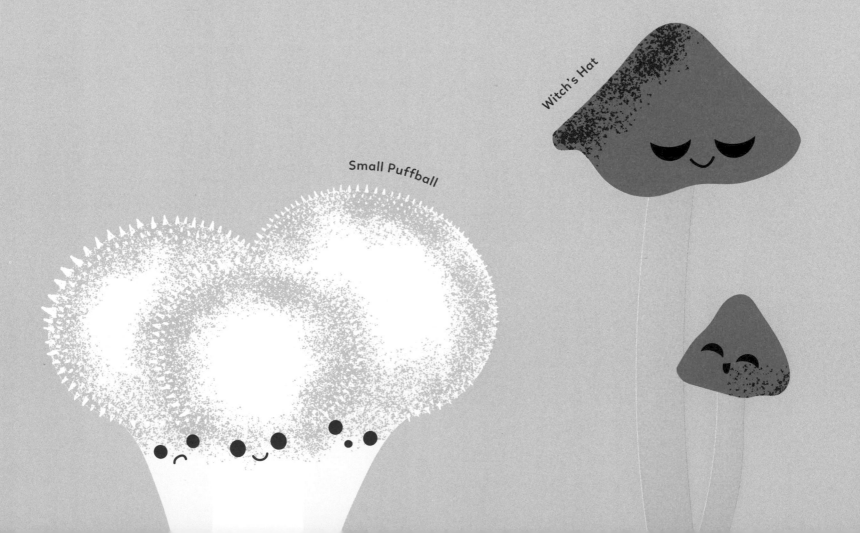

Small Puffball

Witch's Hat

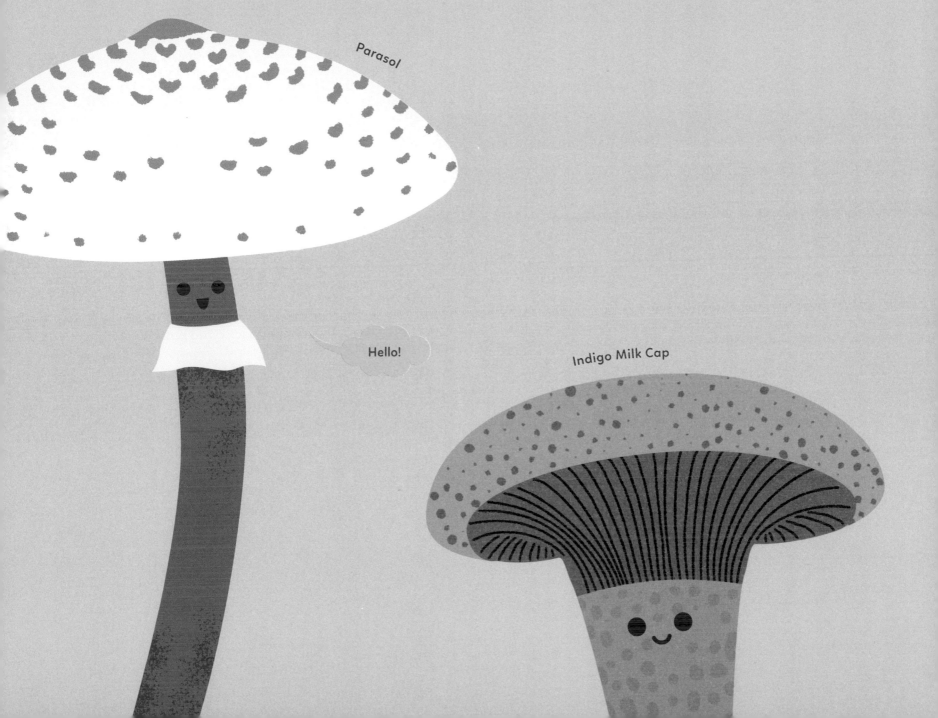

Mushrooms know there is more beneath
the surface than meets the eye.

Yellow Fieldcap

Most of a mushroom is underground in a network called mycelium,
which is made up of living threads of cells known as hyphae.
We only see the top part of the mushroom.

They know that you can stand firm,

yet also spread out free.

Mushrooms make thousands and thousands of spores, which are very tiny and light. These mushroom "seeds" scatter in the wind and find good spots to grow. There are an incredible number of spores in the air, and mushroom spores have been found even in the most remote parts of the world!

Apricot Jelly

Sky-blue

Earthstar

Flame Fungus

Brain

Pink Bonnet

Green Earth Tongue

Mushrooms know that being unique
is a reason to celebrate.

Tongue

Green Elfcup

Fluted Bird's Nest

Eyelash Cup

Octopus Stinkhorn

Chicken of the Woods

Pixie's Parasol

Pink Oyster

Veiled Lady

Blue Chanterelle

Orange Jelly

Parrot Waxcap

Hedgehog

Violet Coral

Mushrooms come in an incredible variety of shapes, sizes, and colors. There are over thirty thousand known species of mushrooms in the world, with more being discovered all the time.

Starfish Stinkhorn

Turkey Tail

Lion's Mane

Bleeding Tooth

Lobster

Giant Puffball

Dog Stinkhorn

Small can be mighty . . .

Inky Cap

Ta-da!

Fly Agaric

Some mushrooms are so strong
they can grow through concrete!
Some are like mini chemical factories
and can produce deadly toxins.

Urk!

Other mushrooms can produce healing remedies like soothing teas, or extracts that aid honeybees.

Reishi

Antler Reishi

Jack-O-Lantern

Who turned
out the lights?

. . . and you can shine
in surprising ways.

Mushrooms know it's fun to glow!

Green Pepe

Honey

Still other mushrooms can glow in the dark!
They are bioluminescent, which means they
produce their own light, like fireflies.
The light mushrooms make is called foxfire.

Eternal Light

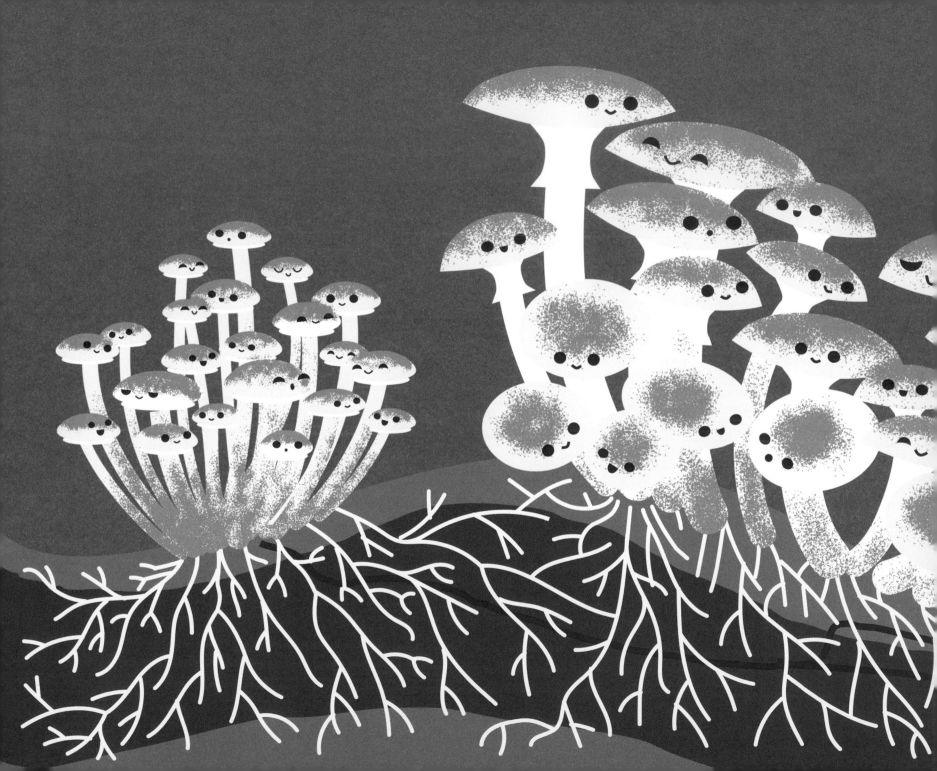

And good to grow!

One honey mushroom has an underground network that covers thousands of acres and has been living for nearly 2,500 years.

Honey

Mushrooms know to grow friendships too.

Many mushrooms are tree helpers. Their underground networks absorb water and minerals and deliver them to trees to help trees grow. The trees give the mushrooms sugar in exchange, which helps the mushrooms grow.

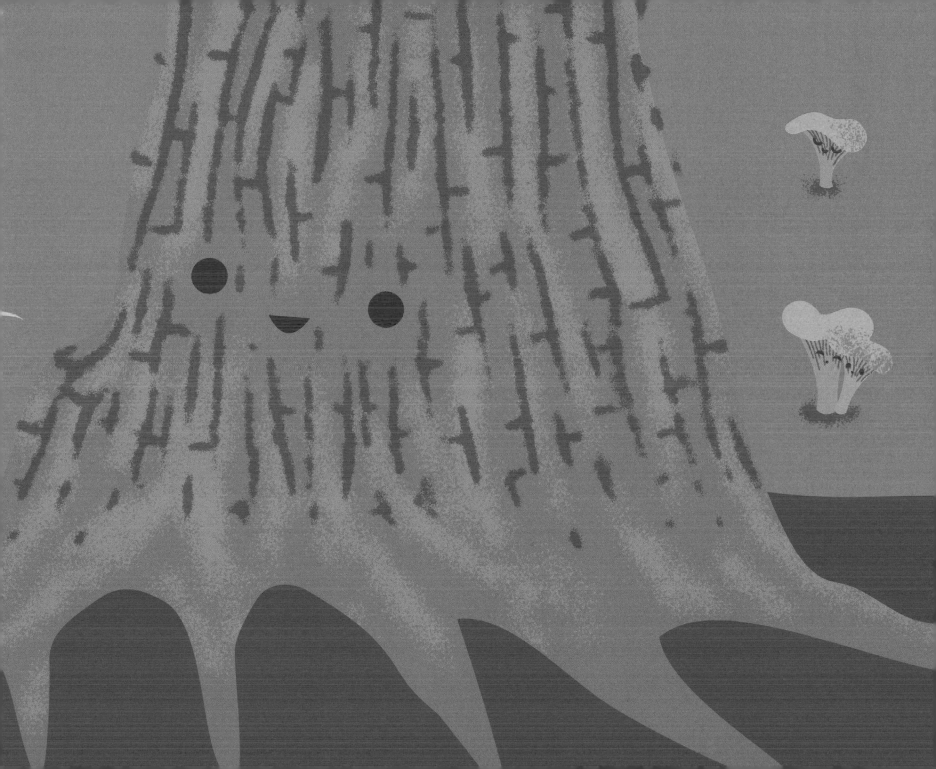

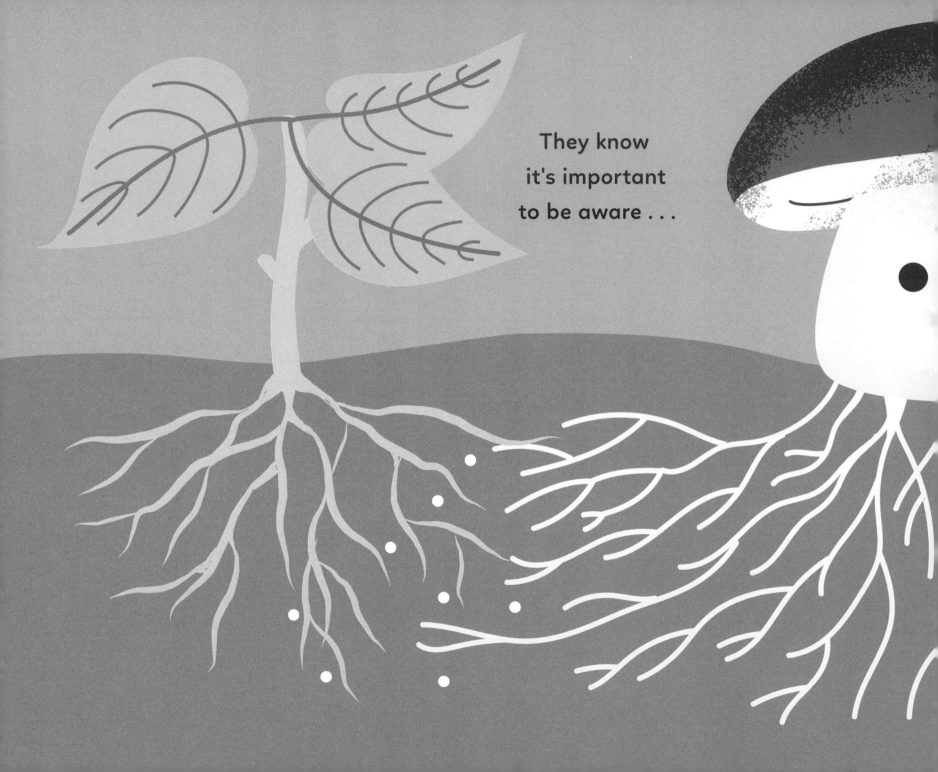

They know
it's important
to be aware . . .

Watch out!

A mushroom's underground network shares chemical messages between itself and its plant partners— for example, if there is a lack of water or an attack by insects!

Porcini

. . . and to take care—
of your neighborhood . . .

Golden Oyster

Unlike green plants that use sunlight to make food, mushrooms get their food in other ways. Many mushrooms break down materials—from dead plants to poop— to get energy. Mushrooms are the ultimate recyclers!

This is DELICIOUS!

Oyster

Hen of the Woods

Mica Cap

. . . and of yourself.

Wine Cap

Wood Ear

Mushrooms look after themselves.
Some mushrooms hibernate over the winter.
They won't grow unless conditions around them are right,
and they can remain dormant (or nap!) for years.
Other mushrooms protect themselves from cold weather
by rolling up into little balls.

Time to sleep . . .

zzzzzzzz

Morel

Morel Sclerotia

Sometimes life can be challenging.

Like for many living things, loss of forests
is devastating for mushrooms.
So is the changing climate, especially droughts.

But mushrooms know to look for opportunities,
to find magnificent ways to carry on.

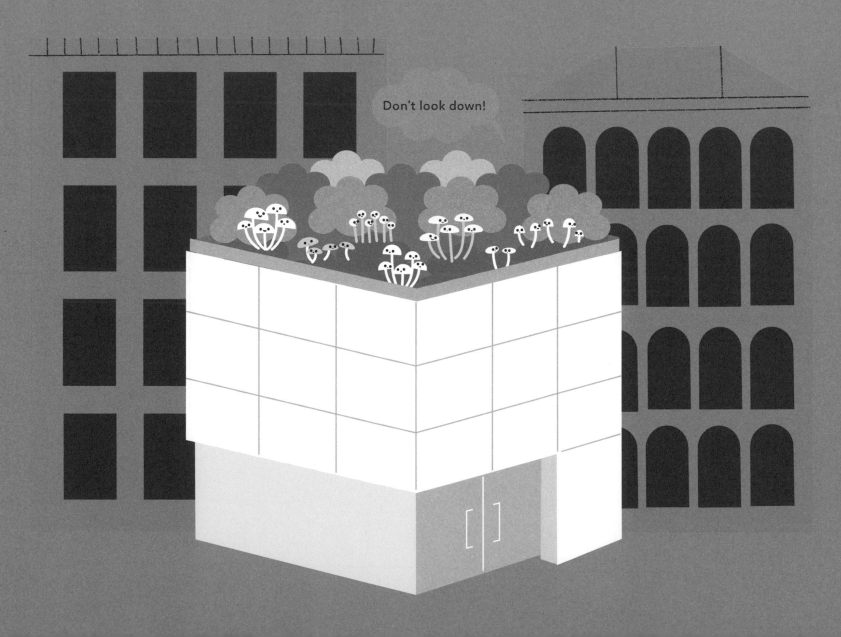

Pinecone Cap

Yay, lightning!

Nameko

Flowerpot Parasol

Mushrooms grow on green roofs in cities, on pinecones, and even in flowerpots inside houses. They can survive forest fires. Studies have shown lightning strikes make some mushroom species multiply.

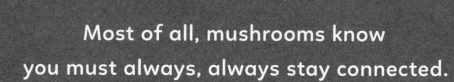

Most of all, mushrooms know
you must always, always stay connected.

That's the way to share—

The more scientists study mushrooms the more they have discovered that mushrooms play a vital role in life cycles and creating healthy ecosystems. We are just beginning to understand all that mushrooms know and do.

with themselves, with others,

and with me and you—

the many things mushrooms know.

Did You Know?

 Mushrooms aren't plants and they aren't animals! They are part of their very own kingdom called the kingdom fungi.

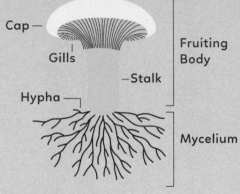

Cap —
Gills
Hypha —
—Stalk
Fruiting Body
Mycelium

Mushrooms are a type of fungus, but not all fungi are mushrooms. Fungi include molds, yeasts, mildews, and more. Mushrooms are a type of fungus that has a large fruiting body above ground.

 Some mushrooms appear overnight. The mushrooms are already there, but they aren't visible. During the night, they fill with water and swell up, like tiny sponge animals that expand into full-size sponges in the bath.

The Fly Agaric is one of the most recognizable mushrooms with its red cap and white spots. Although it's very toxic, it's the toadstool typically pictured in fairy tales.

Oyster mushrooms have been used to clean up oil spills. They can remove chemicals from soil and heavy metals from water through their mycelium, or network of threads.

Bird's Nest mushrooms have fruiting bodies that really do look like birds' nests with tiny eggs. When a raindrop falls into the 'nest,' the mushroom splashes its 'eggs' (which contain spores) through the air to reproduce. Mushrooms are amazing!

What do you know about mushrooms that you can share with your friends?

Remember, mushrooms can be poisonous. It's fun to look for mushrooms, but just look. Never eat or touch any mushrooms you find.

Kallie George is an author and picture book editor who has written numerous acclaimed books for children, including *I Hear You, Forest*; *The Secret Fawn*; and the Heartwood Hotel series. She grew up on the Sunshine Coast in BC, where she spent her days roaming the forests, making up stories, and even looking for mushrooms with her parents. Now, she and her husband have made a home near the woods so that her son can do the same.

Sara Gillingham is an award-winning children's book author and illustrator, art director, and designer who has helped publish many best-selling books. Sara has written and illustrated more than twenty-five titles for children, including *How to Grow a Friend*, *Snuggle the Baby*, the Empowerment series, and the best-selling In My series. She lives in Vancouver with her family.